Cut The B.S

A No Nonsense Guide To Happiness

By Cody Butler

Contents

Dedication

This book is for those who are finished...

Finished dreaming small, finished playing small, finished with mediocrity, finished with quiet desperation and finished with settling for anything less than everything life has to offer.

Most importantly...this book is for those truly finished with being told they can't be happy.

This is a book for those who have decided…

Decided they're stronger than the world

around them, decided never to give in to fear again, decided enough is enough and decided not another day, not another hour, not another minute's going to pass without massive transformation in Happiness, Health, Wealth, And Relationships.

Today is your day...today's the day things change for you. This book is for the Big Dog who's been treated like the underdog...Today is the day your bite is worse than your bark.

Today is the day you take the power back. And lastly, this book is for the committed... Committed to doing whatever it takes to make the change, to make the difference and to being all you're called to be.

I dedicate this book to my beautiful wife Lama who without her continuous support throughout the tough times as well as the good...this work would not exist today.

She has been with me since the very first step of this journey, being my trusted advisor,

Chapter 1

Taking charge

"Many are called, but few are chosen"

Firstly – congratulations on taking action to seek out a better life for yourself. You are now officially in the top 5% of the population! So many are willing to desire more for themselves and others, but few are willing to act – 95% are talkers, 5% are doers. It's no surprise then that 95% of the wealth belongs to 5% of the population! I'm sure the same is true for all good things; the majority is possessed by the few. Let's become one of the few in order that we may educate the masses to the fact that there is enough for all. Being happy, being a winner, being successful and having all good things is scientific. It is available to all who sincerely desire it and are willing to walk the path, follow the steps and open their mind to new experiences. Life is abundant and not limited to only 5%.

Our greatest achievement could well turn out to be grabbing this promise for ourselves and shining our light that others might also find the way. In receiving our desire we also open the path for many others to receive theirs. Becoming happy, successful and fulfilled is your duty.

The achievement of our full potential

The attainment of happiness and all that is contained within it can be rested on one short statement: **the successful achievement of our full potential**. If we accept this to be true, then happiness is not a goal we can pursue directly. The pursuit of happiness actually becomes the pursuit of self development; the continued evolution of the mind, body and soul to the highest level we are individually capable of. Happiness is simply the bi-product of your labour. We can't create happiness; this is not within our power.

However we can create an environment where happiness will show up with unfailing certainty. This works in the same way as creating ice. We can sit forever in front of a bowl of water and sincerely desire for it to turn to ice. However, all the good will and positive thinking in the world will not bring about your goal. The key here is to understand the environment in which water turns to ice. The temperature has to be 0 ºC or less. Create this and nothing else can happen – we will have ice. Very simple! Happiness is the same. Don't sit in front of our bowl of talents, gifts and ambition and just wish and hope.

Create the right environment and our success is assured. As mentioned before, this is scientific; it cannot fail. This book contains the information needed to create that environment.

Now become determined not to rest until we have learnt this information for yourself and successfully assimilated it and applied it to our life.

A few points to bear in mind.

Realistic expectation is essential. We must deal in facts – not what we want it to be, hope for it to be, or wish it was. We need to look at it the way it is.

There are no short cuts – only wise paths.

This book is for those who are serious about themselves and the world they live in. There is no Mac solution to our Mac problems here!

Let's quickly set some realistic expectations.

This is not for the faint of heart, this is tough.

This requires work, dedication and commitment.

Only those with strong motivation and a real

desire to change will succeed.

You must be able to accept a few principles on faith.

The evidence is generally found in the doing.

If we require evidence before engaging in the doing, we are still firmly in the 95%, and not where we want to be.

If this was obvious or logical we all would be doing it! It's not obvious or logical – at least not to begin with. Acting upon faith will allow us to have experiences that those who require evidence will never have. It is in those experiences the answers we all seek lie.

Faith is a must!

This is your life, it's your responsibility.

We may have ten lives to live, who knows? But for right now we've only got one! One chance, one shot – that's it.

Past lives or existence beyond what we know is irrelevant.

The past is just that and the future does not yet exist. Admittedly it is wise to have one eye on the future but essentially we must live and operate in the present.

We must make the most and best use of today.

We have the power now to act upon and bring about any change we choose. History, family, upbringing and education are not relevant and cannot be used as an excuse.

Nobody is responsible for how we act today other than us.

There can be no excuses, only solutions.

We simply cannot allow ourselves to explain problems and obstacles away – they must be overcome.

There is no such thing as excusable failure – there is only failure. Do not allow yourself to become comfortable in procrastination or explaining why a work cannot be completed. Any problem can be overcome if enough time is given to it.

We will encounter problems, when have you ever not? This is life.

Getting good at life means getting good at dealing with problems.

Now that we hopefully have a better understanding of what is required, let's proceed to our first step of taking charge. To understand what I mean by taking charge let's examine our present life situation by making a few statements.

1. **We are the sum total of our past actions.** Everything we have, or are today is a result of our past action. Our job, our car, our house , etc, all results of past action. A loving relationship is a result of a loving past action. Hostility is a result of possibly hostile past actions, or no action at all (still a choice of action). Every physical thing in our lives boils down to a past decision resulting in some kind of action. Our choices may have been limited, or we may even have had no choice at all, but result is

still caused by action. This leads to the cause of those actions.

2. **A decision or choice preceded all action.** All of our past action was chosen by us. Sure, enough pressure can be applied and manipulations used, but even in those situations we still made a choice. We chose between two or more consequences. The fact we felt forced to a particular choice to avoid a certain undesirable consequence does not remove the truth that we still had a choice. To take this one step further, we can see that our decisions or choices had to be preceded by some kind of evaluation or thought process.

3. **Decision or choice is the result of thought.** To be as brief as possible, a

thought or evaluation process had to take place prior to a decision being made. It's what separates us from animals. We have the power to evaluate and make a choice. We can override instinct.

4. **Conclusion - we are what we think.** This is the only conclusion we can arrive at.

Current life = result of past action

Past action = result of past choices and decisions

Choices and decisions = result of our thought process

A different thought process must then produce a different result. What else could happen? The value of this is profound! The next and only logical statement is **change**

our thoughts and we will change your results. This is the foundation of all sustained change of any kind; good or bad. Understand this principle and we are well on your way.

Hopefully we can now see that when I refer to taking charge, I am referring to taking full control of our mind – not bullying or using muscle to control our physical environment. Learning to use our mind in the correct way will certainly give us the results we desire. The challenge now becomes determining what is the correct way? Parents, environment, past experience education, and so on obviously all play a large part in how we think. We have simply accepted what we have been given to be true – not a bad thing. There's no right and wrong here; only results. If what we have been given is not getting the results we desire, look to a new way of thinking. Makes sense – right? The correct way to think is the way that gets us what we want.

Chapter 2

Developing roots

The core of any long-term success in the area of personal development and, thus happiness is the development of a strong belief system. Happiness is like the visible part of an iceberg – it is the part we see and identify with. Similar to the iceberg, happiness is only the tip. Beneath the surface is the main body that actually supports and holds the visible. As mentioned in Chapter 1, happiness itself cannot be created. It is the environment in which happiness exist that we must create. We must grow a deep and strong root system such that we are able to withstand the storms that are inevitably going to come, as well as provide food and nutrients to feed all the necessary functions that will go into providing us with a happy and fulfilled life. These roots are our belief system. It is therefore critical that this task receives or our best attention.

So what is a belief system?

In some respects that's an obvious question – it's what we hold to be true! But it's also far more than that. Our belief system is like our internal compass – it guides us, makes our decisions, determines our level of success or failure – it essentially determines who we are. We all have a belief system; that is not in question. What is in question is: did you choose your belief system, or was it given to you by someone or something else?

More than likely it is probably a little of both. However, if we are to reach our goal we must now take some time and evaluate our beliefs. Be prepared, as this can take time and does require effort. This evaluation can basically be summed up with one question: **"Who am I?"**

To not know who we are is to be lost. To find true happiness whilst being lost is impossible!

We must have a very strong sense of identity if we are to succeed. We must clearly know the answer to this question.

Let's ask a few sample questions to get the ball rolling. Let's not limit ourselves to simply these few questions. The more questions we can ask of ourselves, the better, and the better long-term results we will get. Also the greater depth we can go into, the better results we will get. Remember, our results are always going to be comparative to your efforts. We can have as much or little of life as we choose. If we want more, simply give a little more to the process. So here are a few questions:

· Who am I?

· What are my ethics? In business, in relationships, in my role in society?

· What are my standards on all areas of life that are important to me?

· What do I stand for?

· What will I not stand for?

· What are my spiritual beliefs and convictions?

· What do I love?

· What am I passionate about?

· How do I treat others?

Ask yourself these questions, and as many more as you can think of. Do it in writing. Sit down with a pen and paper and just do it. Take days, weeks, even months if you need to. Once you begin to write, the answers will flow. The longer you write for, the deeper and the higher the quality of answer you will receive. Once you have exhausted your questioning, edit your work. Review it, picking out the most important and striking parts.

When you have gathered this information make a written statement declaring who you are. If you have taken the time to do this correctly, you should have all the information at hand to clearly and concisely write a statement declaring to yourself and the world of who you are! This is ideal, but not actually as far as the statement goes. This is the person you have chosen to be today – not the person you have been in the past. Your past is not relevant.

Here you are determining not only who you are becoming and who you are going to be. **By doing this thoroughly you take a huge step in gaining control of your thoughts,**

and setting course in a direction you choose to go.

Once established, this belief system and statement of identity becomes the back bone of our decision making process. This is our roots, and our compass. It has been consciously and accurately calibrated by us and can be declared reliable.

Congratulations! Measurable progress has been made.

How to best use our belief system for maximum results.

There is good reason we have taken the time to thoroughly develop a workable belief system.

That reason being, **once established, our**

belief system, or value system, becomes the backbone of our decision making processes.

All decisions of any consequence must be measured against our belief system. We cannot violate this belief system by taking action that goes against it. The outcome is not relevant. If, in order to maintain our integrity, we must make a decision that causes an outcome that is not favourable for us – do it anyway.

The long term effects of violating our own beliefs are catastrophic and move us rapidly toward the polar opposite of what we are seeking. To act in a way that knowingly does this is to guarantee pain and is first class foolishness.

What we have established here is also called character and carries many benefits.

As we now know that what we are doing here in our pursuit of happiness is creating an environment in which what we want will grow. This environment is essentially an internal one, or a state of mind to be more precise. Get it right on the inside and everything else on the outside will just show up. It really is that easy! Creating and following our belief system carries many good benefits. A few things we can expect to see as a result of our work are:

· Good health

· A clear conscience - critical to happiness

· High levels of self esteem - critical to happiness

· High levels of confidence - critical to happiness

· Financial, emotional and relationship success

When we have clear set of internal standards we are set free from the need to conform to the standards of others.

We become independent of the good opinion of the 95%. We no longer need their approval. The only standards we need to meet are our own. This allows us to act in ways needed to bring us to our desired goals, and hence the development of confidence and self esteem. A word of warning, it is not that we don't value the approval of others or we don't value their opinion, we simply just don't need it. No need to become arrogant or dismissive of others. This will only slow us down, or even turn us in the wrong direction. Our approval and validation is simply internal and completely self contained. We can confidently act in the face of opposition and still sleep well, knowing we have been true to ourselves –this is a large step in the right direction.

In conclusion, neglect or dismiss this step and our failure is assured. This step must be mastered if we are to receive the maximum benefit from later chapters. Establish a strong belief system and commit to live by it to the best of our ability. If we fall down –

stand up again. The task at hand is a high one – practice and perseverance are the order of the day. Let's be strong, let's continue to move towards all it is that we can be.

If you are not willing to do this, you may as well stop reading.

Chapter 3

Self honesty – the master key

If there is a skill above all others, one key action or process that will bring about more results than any other, then it surely is this – self honesty.

This truly is the master key to unlocking the door to our greatest achievements. A lack of self honesty can be devastating to our life. The man or woman who cannot be honest with themselves lives in a world of denial and delusion. It is through honest dealings and interaction with others that will, to a large extent, provide the physical things that will aid in our happiness. We must first create this honesty within ourselves before we can give it to others in our dealings. Let's be clear, when I say we must be honest, I'm not suggesting that we are all seedy, manipulative liars and cheats, and so forth. I'm just describing the ability to accurately evaluate a situation and to truthfully face the outcome in our minds, even when that truth is very unpleasant. Most of us go to great lengths to avoid the truth, usually in a harmful way. Alcohol and drug addiction are probably the most extreme ways of forgetting or avoiding the truth. Watching excessive amounts of television, video gaming and unproductive literature, are all ways to avoid facing reality. Oversleeping is another great way if you wish to just stick your head in the sand

and ignore all that is going on. There is nothing wrong with any of these things. I'm not suggesting you cut everything out of your life. What you do is your business – just be aware and don't use these past times as a means to procrastinate.

So let's look at some practical points as to why we need to develop this skill. **We have the map to go anywhere we choose to go, but the map is useless without knowing our starting point.** Self honesty will give us this starting point. We need to also uncover and deal with all that has prevented us from becoming happy already.

We must remove the barriers and obstacles that currently exist before we can continue forward. These barriers are generally limited or incorrect beliefs that often revolve around self opinions on matters such as worthiness and self esteem. We will deal with this further in Chapter 6. In order for this to be successful we must have a willingness to be very open with ourselves. Self honesty is the tool with which we will do this work. Our demons must be faced and conquered. The first step in this process is to acknowledge we have these demons – that we have issues. We all do. It's a part of our nature as human beings! If we deny this, we are denying our nature and have much work to do in developing yourself honesty. Denial and delusion are areas we want no dealings with.

This is harmful to us and our plans and has no place in the fulfilled person's life.

In the previous chapter we took time to develop our belief system. This is a great thing, and if done properly, will bring us long-term and lasting benefit. All is in vein if we do not implement this and monitor our thoughts and actions against it in a very candid way. Self honesty then, in a sense, becomes big brother, watching our every action and thought. **It's okay to mess up** – it's going to happen. One of life's ironies is that we are unable to meet even our own standards all the time. **It's not okay to lie to yourself about it.** We can have no interest in explaining our behaviour away to provide ourselves with comfort. This helps nobody, least of all ourselves. No, we must take responsibility for ourselves and accurately label our behaviour. It's black and white. If we fall short in a given task, that's fine. It only becomes failure when we fail to learn from the shortcoming. Life, to a great extent, is a trial and error process; we make a mistake, learn a lesson, a negative is turned into a positive. If, however, we fail in a given task, and then allow ourselves to explain away why we failed – this is failure. A negative has been compounded by adding another negative to it. No lesson has been learned. This is true failure. Therefore it is logical to see that self honesty can in fact turn any situation or circumstance to your benefit, regardless of our physical result. **All chance and luck is removed from the equation of success.**

Applied self honesty can make every single action we take a successful one. If,

as stated in Chapter 1, we are the sum total of our actions, this then leads to only one possible conclusion – do this and failure is impossible.

This is a scientific method and as reliable as gravity. You cannot fail!

Let me review a few key points:

1. We are creating the environment in which happiness can exist and flourish. That environment is an internal one. Nothing external can bring any true happiness without first creating the correct state of mind to receive it. Possessions, property, people and success, and so on, are all valid and good – it's healthy to desire them – but only when desired with the correct mindset. Create the right internal environment and we can have all these good things added to you. If we first seek the material, we probably will never have it, and if we do, well, it will become our greatest source of misery. This is why we behave in a way that benefits us internally, even if it costs us dearly in the short-term.

2. Monitor your motivation, not just your action. A successful outcome undertaken under the wrong motivation is failure. Be aware; very aware of this. In the short-term, you can get what you want quicker and easier than the method laid out before you. However, the key word in the method presented to you here is **sustained** – long term, sustained happiness. This is what this method offers. Do not be tempted like the fools; **all that shines is not gold.** You can get big money by working in immoral industry; you can develop self esteem by belittling others; you can gain social advantage by being the spreader of lies and rumours. All these can provide short-term benefit. However, the end result of all is poverty and misery. **There are no shortcuts**. Again we are dealing with laws of science. Failure is as scientific as success. **Do not be tempted.** Make sure your motivation to action is as honest as your desire to achieve results.

3. Don't be harsh with yourself. Always speak to yourself in a kind and loving way. You're going to make mistakes; this is a given. When it happens, learn the lesson, make the necessary correction and move on, knowing that you are now closer to your goal than you were before the mistake. Again be honest. Let your criticism be constructive and useful. Harsh, non constructive criticism is no more than a form of self harm. It does not help you or anybody – it's not needed, don't do it. Correction is good and is needed, so let's just be smart about it.

4. Monitor your thoughts constantly. I just can't say this too many times. Develop the habit of self awareness.

We are now ready for the next step.

Chapter 4

Eliminating negativity

The quickest and most efficient way to bring shipwreck to an otherwise seaworthy vessel, is to laden it with a cargo of negativity.

Negativity is precisely what the word says – it's negative. It is the fastest and most assured way to drive all good things away from you and attract disaster back into your life. **We are what we think, and what we are is what we attract.** Therefore what we think is what we attract – simple as that. This is a natural law of the universe that does not discriminate and can fail. **We are what we think.** I really cannot repeat this enough. It logically follows that if all our thoughts are good, and only of what we want, then we must, by the laws of science, attract to us what is good and only what we want. Think about this at an observable level; birds of a feather do flock together; an honest man will not attract the friendship of thieves. A capitalist will not attract the companionship of communists. People who like to moan, complain and generally despise all they have in life will only be able to maintain the company of other like-minded individuals. A grateful, enthusiastic soul would quickly remove themselves from such company – they would find it draining! Misery loves company; this is true. Equally true and much less quoted, is the fact that so does happiness!

It is not enough that we desire to be happy, we must act in a way that allows us to attract the people and resources into our lives that will encourage and teach us the path to happiness.

These people we seek to attract are happy to help, happy to share their knowledge, happy to give their experience, happy to freely give of all of their resources and time and happy to lead by their example. Do you see something here?

They are happy, happy to…happy to… happy to.

These lucky people find happiness is every act of contribution. There is no obligation, no pressure and no self benefit.

These people give simply because they are happy to give.

We must attract these people into your life if we are to succeed. They will teach us the way. This book and any other book can only go so far. We need role models – people who know the way – so that may follow.

So knowing this, the question again then becomes, "How must we think in order to attract what it is that we need?"

We must learn to think in a habitually positive way.

Now let me qualify this. When I say think in a positive way, I am not referring to the 'happy, clappy, I think I can, I think I can, school of thought'. No, let's get this clear.

This might well be excellent, but it's not what I am referring to. When I refer to positive thinking I mean…

1. Always see the good in situations and people. There is always a benefit to be gained and a lesson to be learnt. Every situation and person carries this gift with them. We do not have to like the person or the circumstance, we do not have to enjoy it; we just have to learn from it. Our greatest adversaries carry with them the potential to be our greatest teachers. Let's look for this and use it to our advantage. **When we encounter resistance, do not become negative – get excited.** This alone will change our lives. How many of the 95% welcome trouble?

2. Don't ignore the bad – that's called stupidity – just don't dwell on it. As we learnt in the last chapter, we must accurately and honestly evaluate all situations. We can't pretend; that's not the game we are playing. When what's less that desired is presented before us we have to acknowledge that, in order to make good, sensible decisions. The key here is just not to dwell on it. Make it a small part of a bigger picture, not the main attraction. What we focus on grows. Let's make sure what we grow is good!

3. Look for empowering meanings in every situation. Events themselves are meaningless; they are neither good nor bad. One man's joy is another man's misery. Some people are happy rich, some are happy poor, some are happy married, some happy single; get my point. The reverse is also true in all accounts.

Events do not carry happiness or sadness in themselves. It is what an event means to us that determines how we react to it.

That meaning is determined by us. This again is another life changing statement that if we can grasp it and apply it, it will transform us to the next level of evolution. **We must find empowering meaning in every situation.**

To quote Dr Wayne Dyer "change the way we see things, and the things we see will start to change". Look for meaning that strengthens and helps us – not the opposite. Looking for the negative meaning is a completely self defeating act and the action of a fool!

4. Think the best in the absence of evidence. Stop making statements like "I just know" – you don't know. In thinking negatively of a situation before you know the outcome, we are far more likely to take action that will bring about a negative outcome by our own hand. We will become a self fulfilled prophecy. We will, in fact, become a self fulfilled prophecy either way – let's just make sure we are prophesying good things. By thinking the good, we just use this same fact to your advantage. Makes sense? **In the absence of evidence think the best.** Think people like you, think you did well at a job interview, think people's motivation is good. Why think badly when there is no more, or no less reason to think good. **Stop road blocking yourself** for no good reason...we might be pleasantly surprised at the outcome.

5. Never speak bad of people...say nothing. This is basic stuff. Speaking bad, even if justified, is negativity. The people we need in our life are not going to be attracted to this. When we speak badly of one to another it brings about the question of how does this person speak of me when I am not around? If we must speak of somebody in such a way, make sure that the person being spoken of is present, and given the opportunity to explain and defend their position. This is best avoided altogether though. Disputes happen, of course. When they do, deal directly with the parties involved. Do this in private, not public – do not turn the situation into gossip and public news.

6. Be independent of the good opinion of others. We do not seek approval outside of ourselves. This is why we spent time developing a belief system. This is our measuring stick. It has been said **we can please some of the people all of the time, or all of the people some of the time. We cannot please all of the people all of the time.** This is true enough. If we need to please, we are setting ourselves up to fail. Our own approval is the only approval needed to be happy. That's not to say we don't seek to please, of course we do, or that we don't value the opinion of others, again, of course we do. We just don't **NEED** it in order to be happy.

The same word of warning here again as before. Do not become arrogant in this lack of need of approval. We do this quietly and without fuss. Never tell people you don't care what they think, or you don't need them. Unless of course you're just trying to alienate them from your life.

7. Do not moan or whine about what you cannot change. We could even go one step further and say do not moan or whine… period. It's not attractive in any way at all. If we cannot change a situation, we can change your view of that situation. This is the successful action. **Complaining simply adds fuel to the fire.** Accept what we cannot change – we have no choice. Use the step described previously; find a new meaning and learn a lesson. If we are to succeed, we need people around us who possess the ability to solve problems. All problem solvers know that moaning is not a solution to any problem. To attract these people, we ourselves must develop good problem solving skills. Start this process by eliminating this negative behaviour from our lives.

Remember it is an internal environment we are creating here. Our external life is no more than a mirror reflection of what is going on inside. Having said this, let's raise a few points to carefully consider:

· Never, ever turn negativity inward on yourself

· Monitor self talk closely and constantly

· Never curse yourself

· Never put yourself down

· Never agree with yourself that a task is impossible; all things are possible

· Never doubt yourself

· Never speak to yourself in a way you would not allow others to speak to you

Our opinion of ourselves will almost exclusively determine the opinion others have of us – make sure it's a good one.

In conclusion, we will attract to us what we are. If we are inwardly or externally negative, we will begin a cycle of attracting negative people and events towards us, who will slow down, halt or even reverse our progression toward happiness. Conversely, adopting a positive persona will attract those who are willing, able, and happy to expedite our process. Changing our thinking is not easy. It takes time and practice, but it can be done, and must be done. Look around you. The people that have a place in our life are going to be an accurate measure of who we are. As we see more and more happy, successful people coming onto our path, this is a good sign that we are moving in the right direction.

One last point: the ultimate in positive thinking is the **abundance consciousness.** Know there is an abundance for all; plenty to go around. We can give freely because we have received freely. We can never run out. We don't have to hoard or compete over resources or opportunity. This is the **scarcity consciousness** and is the ultimate in negative thinking. Leave the competition for the 95%. We have only one competitor to overcome and that's ignorance! If we succeed in this we will be free from the tyranny of scarcity for ever and free to enter into the abundance that is life.

Chapter 5

Understanding the power of language

In the beginning was the word,

and the word was with God and the word was God.

(John 1:1)

The Universe in which we live was created by words, spoken into existence. Words are far more than just sounds coming from our mouths. Words carry creative power. This same creative power and ability that was used to create all has been imparted into each one of us. We all have it, and we all use it whether we are aware of the fact or not. Let's become aware and use this to our advantage. Let's briefly compare humans with the animal kingdom. Animals do not have the use of words or a cohesive language.

So then what is the animal kingdom's greatest achievement on the plain of creation – nothing! Not a building, not a book, not one work of art, not a single space craft – nothing. Humans, on the other hand, have both words and language. What is our greatest achievement? Well take your pick. Let me say here, our ability to create is not limited to good; we also carry the ability to create great bad. I'm not suggesting we have used this power wisely, I am simply demonstrating that we have used it. So why, in this sense, have we far out performed the animal kingdom? It's because we have the use of words – words are the raw material of creation.

Without the effective use of language we are very limited in our ability to do anything on the creative plain. I realise this might be a little far fetched for some at this point, but stay with me and I will explain further. There is great benefit to be gained here.

Your world is spoken into existence by you.

Let be clear, creators is what we are aiming to become here. We are aiming to create an environment where happiness can grow, our wants and needs are provided for in a most acceptable way, and our reality is in perfect in harmony with both our own desires, and those of the world around us. By becoming creators and co-creators with the source of original substance, we take charge of our lives and take a huge step in the right direction. By grasping this concept and making best use of it, we enter into the reality that we have the ability to create. **We can have anything we want,** so long as it does not harm or interfere with the path of another. Our tool in this creation process is words. Let me state a few facts about words:

1. Words have power. Hopefully this will become evident as you read on.

2. Words are things. Again probably not the most logical to some, but just keep this in mind. Soon, you will hopefully see the truth of this.

3. Words are yours forever; once spoken they can never be taken back. Make every effort to understand the implications of this. It sounds obvious and it is, but all too often you forget it. Be slow to speak. Be slow to anger. Think about what you are about to say and the long term consequence of your words. The results of speech are quite often permanent. Be aware that all kind of emotions have the ability to temporarily steal our clarity. A word spoken in anger can change your life forever – in a bad way. Learn self control. Learn to recognise when your mind is not clear, and refrain from speaking at that time. If you are to be happy you need smooth relationships with those around you. Learn when it is wise not to speak, and gain the control to not do so. **If ever in doubt as to what to say, say nothing.** Silence is easy to explain at a later point – many other things are not!

4. Words carry consequence. By understanding this we can start to see the logic of our first two statements. Use words to insult somebody's religious or political views and you may well start a war. Many wars have begun over nothing more than words. How many men have had their lives taken from them simply for words spoken either for or against a particular cause? Insult the wrong person's family with your words and you may meet with a less than pleasant response. Humanitarians have used words to inspire millions to action, thus changing the world for the better. Tyrants have used words to divide nations and cause untold bloodshed and misery. Words are indeed powerful things. Once you understand this power, you can start to harness it and use it to our best advantage. All you need do is pick your desired consequence, then find the words that bring that about – very simple.

5. Words create love. Pretty essential if you are going to be happy. How you speak to another will largely determine how they feel about you. Kind, loving words will create kind, loving relationships. Harsh, cold words will create harsh, cold relationships. This is obvious. Can you now start to see how it is that we speak our world into existence?

6. You can instantly bring joy or upset to virtually anybody with words. Give a sincere compliment to another and watch what happens. You can make a complete stranger's day with nothing more than a few well chosen words. The same is true with the opposite. You can ruin somebody's day with a carelessly spoken word.

7. What you want you must communicate to others. The easiest and best way to do this is show them what you want by giving it to them. By finding every opportunity to encourage and support others with our words, you will begin a cycle of attracting this same encouragement back in let's be sure that you give it away generously. **Do not be stingy with your good words**, unless that's what you want back!

DO NOT underestimate the power of words and language.

Words begin as thoughts. So again we arrive back at our basic premise. All things begin as thought – we are what we think. After the thought has initially occurred we then make the decision to speak.

Essentially, this decision is action. We then speak using words and language. Once a word has been spoken, it adopts the form of its physical equivalent, thus becoming a thing. This physical form then becomes our reality. We speak our world into existence. Probably the two most powerful words in this process are **"YES"** and **"NO".** These two words possibly change our reality quicker than any other. For example, if you are asked if you would like coffee and you say yes, your word almost instantly takes the form of its physical equivalent; in this case coffee. Your word becomes a thing and that thing becomes your reality. If you say no, your word again becomes it physical equivalent and you receive a completely different reality. A simple example, but multiplied out, this is true at all levels. Words are things.

This is the next piece of the puzzle. We begin as thought, thought becomes action (or words) and our words become things; these things then become our reality. We control this entire process of creation.

Remember, this is science; it cannot fail. Keep in mind we are seeking to create an environment here, not physical objects. Material things will come, but for now we only need this principle for the purpose of creating our environment.

· Use loving words and we will create a loving environment

· Use hostile words and we will create a hostile environment

Words will always create the form of their physical equivalent. Rarely, if ever, do hostile words take the form of a loving, physical reality, and visa versa. See my point yet? Now we know this, let's take full advantage by looking at a few things we should speak of freely and often:

1. Speak health into your life and into the lives of others. Remember our words will take the form of their physical equivalent. We must only speak of what we want. Good health is essential to happiness. We can all have it, regardless of how we are at present. Start by telling how well you are. Chapter 7 will cover more on this.

2. Speak of joy, love and patience. We are going to need all of these, so let's get the ball rolling by talking about them.

3. Speak of success, wealth and prosperity. We want it all! Don't be embarrassed because we want wealth and prosperity in your life. This is noble and right. Our greatest gift to the world is to live life to the fullest, and to teach others how to do the same. We need physical resources to do this. As happy people, we live in the abundance consciousness; there is no of it lack here. When the supply is limitless, our rightful and fair share of this is everything. Have as much as we can carry, then come back for some more! **Think it, speak it, become it. 1-2-3** – Basic maths!

4. Speak Happiness. Obviously. Let's no longer mentally class ourselves with what we once were, or what have no desire to be. Let our thoughts, actions and words be congruent and consist in support of our chosen path. Let them be deliberate and decided by us.

5. Do speak of how well you are doing. Don't hide your light so as not to remind others of their own failure. The greatest thing you can do for these people, the 95%, is to show them by your example, that they too can have it all. If people are offended by your success, distance yourself from them. They can't help you, and you can't help them. They are asleep. Maybe one day they will wake, and you will offer our help, but for now –move on.

6. Be proud of your achievement and speak of grander success to come. This is only right. All you have is a result of your diligence and hard work. By being proud of your achievements you are essentially displaying gratitude for what you have been given. **Gratitude is the currency of happiness.** To deny your success and achievement is essentially to be ungrateful –

don't do it. Now when I say be proud, I don't mean be boastful or arrogant and belittle others by your success – not at all. Simply take a day's wages for a day's work. Gratefully receive the fruits of your labour – it's only right. Healthy people, the kind of people we need to surround ourselves with, will take joy in our joy. If your success offends, again, move on, as these people can't help you.

Finally, monitor our inward conversation. Use words in the same way to create our internal state. Remember what's on the inside will reflect its mirror image on the outside. It all begins with the inner game.

Chapter 6

Uncovering Limiting beliefs

The next step on our journey is now to uncover and remove any obstacles blocking our path and preventing us from getting what it is we really want.

Most of the time, our biggest obstacle is, ironically – ourselves, or, more precisely, our limiting beliefs about ourselves. We have developed a belief system already that states who we are and what we are. We have taken the time to choose those beliefs and decided deliberately who we want to be. This is good work. We cannot stop here though. We must now also uncover and remove our remaining beliefs that do not support the person we are becoming, and the life that we are moving towards. What we believe to be true must be consistent with what we do not believe true. If it is not, we will fail.

So what is a limiting belief? We shall say that it is this: **a thought or idea that we hold to be true, that limits or halts our progress towards the achievement of our goals.** Accept on faith that we are no limit creatures. Our potential is limitless. We can have all we want, and we can be we want. If you cannot accept this as true, then this in itself is a limiting belief for you. **We can never have what we do not believe to be true.** We can have a genuine desire for anything we choose, but if we do not hold the attainment of it as being possible, then we shall never have it. If you can accept this as true, then uncovering and removing these blocks is going to be considerably easier. **All things are possible;** this is our attitude. It is not enough to say it; we must know it, deep, deep inside. The proof of this comes and roots develop when we conquer seemingly impossible tasks. When the impossible becomes possible, we then know this to be true. It is this belief that drives us to take on the impossible, without it we could never find the motivation to even try, let alone succeed. Adopt the truth that all things are possible and watch our livese transform before our very eyes!

Happiness is dependant on the constant setting and achieving of goals.

Being happy is not dependant on material things, although we will certainly have these things if we are happy. By the constant setting and achieving of worthy goals we accomplish several things that are critical to our success. Let me demonstrate:

1. We find purpose. To start with, it is very small, but when we set even the smallest of goals in the beginning, our movement and actions become purposeful. We become deliberate and self controlled and we purposefully move toward the goal we have set. As we gain skill in this area, our goals become bigger and more focused, our successes grow and our purpose becomes more defined. If we continue this process to its conclusion, our ultimate purpose is found. Not only that, but when we do discover it, the cumulative achievements leading up to this point will have provided us with the tools, resources and skills needed to effectively meet the physical needs our ultimate purpose will require of us. This is the process. **Find your purpose in life and you are certainly on the right road.**

2. We develop confidence and self esteem. Constantly setting and achieving goals brings immense confidence and self esteem. When we know in ourselves that we will do what we say we will do, and when we know we will achieve our goals with confidence, it allows us to act with confidence.

Every act of confidence in an individual is added to the previous, confidence grows and larger tasks can be attempted and overcome.

It is the feeling of purpose, and the feeling of confidence that will contribute greatly to our happiness. This feeling alone is enough; this is an internal world we are creating. Fortunately we have science on our side, and any person acting in a purposeful and confident way can do nothing other than generate material success. Hopefully, we see now that if we are happy all good things have no choice but to show up in our life. I don't want to cover goals too much at this point they are discussed in detail in Chapter 9. I am just demonstrating that how **a belief that prevents us from the setting and achieving of goals is going to be very detrimental to our success.**

So how do we overcome limiting beliefs? This first step is self awareness. I may be repetitive here, but this is a master key to so many things. We cannot correct what we do not realise to be incorrect – this is obvious. We must begin by taking an honest inventory of ourselves and we must know what we want. Clarity is the key. Mixed feelings bring about mixed results. We don't want mixed results; we want clear results in areas of our choosing. The only way to achieve this is through mental clarity. Get clear; get clear results. **Saying I don't know what I want is not acceptable.** To say I don't know, is to say I want nothing. This is precisely what you will get – nothing. If you have not found purpose and direction yet, this is fine. I don't want to beat anybody up. It's not the easiest thing, but we must be devoting a considerable about of our resources into figuring this out. No plan equals no results. If we have no goals and no direction, then our first goal is to have a goal and have a direction. This is a good start. We have purpose now – to find purpose. Remember, this is a process that builds. Don't feel you need all the answers at once; you only ever need the next answer, and a new question. This is within the scope of all who seek it. This may take years, but that's fine. As long as we are making steady progress in the right direction we will ultimately find what it is we are looking for.

Our biggest limiting belief is our sense of self worth. This is where yourself honesty really comes in to its own. We must, with complete honesty, ask ourselves how worthy am I to receive what it is that I desire?

Most, if not all, have self worth issues at some level. To admit to ourselves that we do not feel worthy, we do not feel capable and confident, we do not feel deserving of our hearts desire or we do not feel like a worthwhile and contributing member of society and so on is very, very difficult. Most of us just tend to bury these feelings, ignore them and exist in a state of denial. By denying these feelings we successfully avoid dealing with them. Sadly we also avoid all the greatness and joy life has to offer. It is our true feelings towards ourselves that determine precisely how much or how little of life we have. We can never receive physically what we do not feel worthy of internally. Increase your sense of self worth and your ability to receive life increases accordingly. We will always receive all we are capable of receiving; this is a fact. **Life wants to give.**

Essentially it is those beliefs about ourselves that can be most harmful. Fortunately, if we get this right we can use it to our advantage. Have a limited belief and you will have a limited outcome. Turn that belief into an unlimited belief and you will have the world before you! This theme will continue throughout the upcoming chapters. Hopefully, you can also see how it has equally been part of the preceding ones. There is no one solution to this. **Continued personal development is the key – seek it constantly**.

However, let's begin by exploring a few

steps that are helpful in overcoming these obstacles:

Step 1. Take action.

Taking the time to work through the previous chapters is really key.

It's not enough to just become aware of information– this changes very little. It is our action upon this information that will bring about positive change. The 95% talk, 5% do. This doing is essentially the only difference between super achievers and very mediocre achievers. No particular gifts, attributes, social privilege or intellectual advantage is needed.

Learn the information – take action. That's it. If you don't agree with the information presented here, seek other literature and ideas; **just take action** of some kind. The Chinese proverb "a journey of a thousand miles begins with one step" is so true here. Everything you need to succeed will be provided at the appropriate time – just take that first step. Having read far enough to even read these words is a good sign you are ready; most will have quit by now. Just keep going!

Step 2. Review step one and repeat!

Seriously. I make no claims in my ability to hold the answers. My only claim is that I have been able to find and gather the information that I needed for myself. I happily share what I have found, but each each individual's needs are different. No one solution will work for all. What will work for all is the fact that the knowledge we each seek is available – At least for those who take the time to look! What we need here goes beyond one book, one author and one series of facts.

Commit to yourself to make your own personal development a priority, take action daily, and you will succeed. The steps and processes you individually need will be revealed to you as the time becomes right. Again, act on faith. Know you will get what you want and you surely will get it.

Step 3. Closely and honestly examine our attitudes about ourselves.

How do you feel about yourself? Ask yourself searching questions. As we have already mentioned, your answers will determine your physical reality. If you do not feel worthy of love, you will not have it. If you feel you do not have any skills that warrant more than minimum wage, you will not make more than minimum wage.

If you think of yourself as slow and unintelligent, you will behave in a way that convinces others that you are slow and unintelligent. **We must know how we truly feel about ourselves to progress.** Once these limiting beliefs are out and on paper we can then set to work on changing them.

Henry Ford summed this up beautifully when he said **“whether you think you can, or whether you think you can’t, you’re right”.**

What you think becomes your reality.

Step 4. Set to work on changing any belief that does not serve and support you.

Use the information contained in the previous chapters and the chapters to come – all the information given is useful. A good value system, positive use of language, mental discipline, goal setting, and an accurate self examination are all required. Sadly there is no one sentence I can write here that will fix everything at once. We simply must change the way we think – probably the hardest work known to man! Persevere, the results are worth it.

Step 5. Be realistic about the time required.

This probably will not happen in a day. A

three to five year goal to bring about positive and lasting change is realistic. Of course we will see continued improvement throughout, but time is required. We are sowing seeds here; they need time to grow and they must be tended to while they grow. We need patience. Don’t be discouraged if things don’t happen at once – that’s one of the biggest lies of western culture. As long as is needed is as long as it will take.

Chapter 7

Feel great about anything

Circumstance, events and peoples actions all fall outside of our area of control, and so they should, just as our actions fall outside of the control of others.

Luckily for us, happiness is a feeling and not an event or person. Events cannot be controlled, but how we feel about those events can. **Feeling is everything.**

Everything we desire, we desire for one reason only; how it makes us feel. This is why the same thing has different effects on different people. One might buy a house and be very happy because it brings a feeling of security. Another may be in possession of the same house but very unhappy, why? It brings about a feeling of a loss of freedom. A house is a house, neither happy nor sad; the difference is the meaning applied to the house and the consequent feelings that meaning produces.

When we understand it is feelings that we want, then the fact we have no control of most things outside of ourselves becomes irrelevant. We simply need to learn ways to feel great about anything – this is possible. We have the ability to generate feelings about anything. **How you feel is a choice.** Now let's be sensible here, some things in life are going to make us sad, for example, the loss of loved ones or the diagnoses of illness. Grief is appropriate; a period of sadness is appropriate.

Let's not go to extreme examples that occur once every ten or twenty years to prove this wrong. I'm talking about day to day life. Let me explain further how we choose our feelings.

Feelings are generated by our thoughts. We can only feel an emotion whilst we hold a thought of what is causing that emotion in our mind. Ever been sad or upset about something, become distracted for while and felt good for a bit. Then later we remembered we were upset, changed our thoughts back to what had upset us, and thus become upset again?

Of course, we all have. That is why good

friends will try to distract us when we are upset – it helps. **We can only feel what we focus on.**

How we focus is our choice. **Change how you think and you will change how you feel.**

Obviously I am making sweeping statements here that are easy to say and harder to do, but I am simply trying to demonstrate the truth of the situation – the fact that how we feel is a choice. The "hows" will come shortly.

So we have now gone full circle and can only logically arrive back at our original conclusion –that we are what we think. We can again make a series of statements to demonstrate this further.

· We are what we think

· What we think determines how we feel

· What we think is our choice, thus how we feel is our choice

· Change our thought, change our feelings, change our reality

Don't forget that we will attract to us what we are. If we are sad, we will tend to use sad words, which will in turn adopt their physical sad equivalent, and thus begin a cycle of attracting more sadness back into our lives.

We must break the cycle of negative patterns and replace them with positive cycles. The achievement of this and our ultimate success can then be summed up in the successful accomplishment of one goal: **We must develop the discipline to take full control of our thoughts.**

If we do this we will have control of our lives, our achievements, our purpose and of course, our happiness. We will become creators with the ability to create any reality we choose. Nothing will be beyond us and all things will be possible to us. We can have whatever we want, and as much of it as we want. We will truly be in a position to live life to our fullest potential. Everything offered in this book is to the ends of gaining control of our thoughts, thus allowing us to share in all the good things just described.

Through out this life-long process of taking control, we are assuredly going to encounter resistance. The untrained mind is like a child and is surely going to rebel at the prospect of discipline – you are in for a fight! Your mind and your ego are not going to like being told what to do by you one little bit! It is going to fight, kick and scream. As I mentioned before, if this was easy, everybody would be doing it. They are not, look around, what you see tells this story for itself. If we are to be exceptional then it stands to reason that the lengths we must go to must also be exceptional. Never did 2 + 2 = 100. The maths always adds up. We get what we give.

Now to the hows – how we feel about things. It essentially it boils down to this:

· Get clear about how you want to feel about

a person, or circumstance. Remember, clear thoughts = clear results

· Ask yourself the question, "If I felt how I want to feel about XYZ, how would I act?"

· Act in that way. Simply use discipline to guide you action

It will feel strange at first, even uncomfortable, but if you persist your thoughts will very quickly become consistent with your actions. You will begin to feel in accordance with your action. We cannot think one way and act another –not long-term anyway. This would violate the fact that we are what we think. No, the way we act, and the way we think will always line up. It may take a short period of time for this to happen, but it will happen.

For this to work successfully we must employ all we have learnt so far. Once we have determined how we wish to feel, we must use language that supports those chosen feelings. Telling ourselves we love our job, then saying we hate it, then saying we love it, and so on, is a waste of time. It will not work. If we do in fact dislike our job but want to love it, use only language that speaks of that. Show up early, maybe stay late. Tell our employers how much you appreciate the opportunity. Act in a way that somebody who loved that job would act. Pretty soon we will love it. This works every time.

Again, we cannot always control our circumstances, or the job we may well have to have –at least for now. Though, we can choose how we feel about that job. Just think, is an employee who is positive, enthusiastic, diligent and reliable, more or less appealing to a future employer with a better job and more money, than somebody who is down, negative and belittling of what they currently have? Obviously. At the very least we will attract a better job! If we want more, become deserving of more – simple.

Discipline is required here. What we are doing is overriding our nature to some extent, or at least our nurture.

Be warned, it is going to feel wrong and we're not going to want to do it – do it anyway. **It is what separates the exceptional from the exceptionally average!** This is what discipline and self control are.

They are like muscles and only become strong by being exposed to progressively increased resistance. No pain, no gain. Remember there are no short cuts. So now we have our basic method, let's add a few points to keep in mind that may be useful.

· Thoughts are like seeds; plant a seed of increase, water it with constant supportive language, feed it with positive action, and watch it grow into a strong tree of abundance…clever! We are going to plant seeds regardless – just make sure they are good ones.

· Stop watering bad seeds. Just let the birds eat them.

· Use only constructive language that supports our purpose.

Lastly, a word of caution. Make sure any negative attitudes are not bringing about benefit. Some people develop negative states because it gains them sympathy or profit of some kind. The same desired results can be brought about in a healthy way. We must be honest in our examination of our motives here.

Chapter 8

The internal thermostat

Our beliefs, or more accurately yourself beliefs, quite simply are going to determine the level of success we will achieve in every area of life. This is why we have spent time on building a belief system, as well as spending time on removing limiting beliefs.

These beliefs can be looked at as a thermostat.

The level of success that is physically present in our lives can temporarily go up or down, but our internal thermostat (our subconscious) will soon bring us back to our pre-determined setting. Fortunately for us we determine that setting.

By increasing our settings we increase our ability to receive. If somebody offers us 10 litres of water, but we only have only a 1 litre container, no matter how badly we want the water, we have no capacity to receive it. View life in this way. Life is willing to give far more than we ask, or could ever use – it is our lack of ability to receive that limits us. Most, if not all, desire more. It is not desire we lack, it is the capacity to receive our desire. What we must then do is increase our ability to receive. This goes hand in hand with a willingness to ask. To desire something is not the same as to ask for it. We must feel it is right that we ask of life, and we must feel worthy to receive what we have asked for. Get this right and we can't go wrong! We ask in the form of goals, which will be covered in the next chapter. Here, we will work on creating a place to put what we have asked for when it shows up. We must have a means to appropriate what is ours as it comes to us.

We cannot receive happiness, or anything else, without first believing that we deserve it. What we truly believe we deserve is what we will get. It really is that basic. This is our thermostat setting. Here is a fact –**we all deserve it!** That includes you, that includes me, and that includes everybody. We deserve it by virtue of the fact we are. All men and women are created equal. We are given one thing, and one thing only, that is solely ours – the ability to think.

This ability carries within it everything needed to create any life we choose. Some use it wisely; most squander it.

Happiness and success are not privileges that we must earn, they are our birthright.

We just have to receive it. Let's not make this harder than it is.

If we can grasp the concept that we were born worthy of all that we want, this will make things a lot easier. Let me qualify this; when I say we do not have to earn our worthiness, I do not mean we do not have to work, we do. What I mean is our worth as a human being cannot be earned. It is free. We could view this inherited worth as unlimited potential, what we do with that potential depends entirely on us.

Do not listen to people who tell us contrary to this. To believe that all are worthy, including us is to truly believe the best of everybody.

This is honourable and noble. It is quite legitimate to have this opinion of ourselves when we extend the same privilege to all. To think of ourselves as worthy, whilst believing others to be not worthy, or visa versa, would be no more than passing judgement. We have no right or ability to do this. As I stated in the opening chapter, **to become happy and fulfilled is our duty.** Why? Because in order to accomplish this we must know all are equal and that all are worthy; simply by birthright. Once we fully grasp this, then we are in a position to begin contributing to the betterment of all. This contribution is our purpose; it is why we are here. **If we find our purpose and we act upon it, we will have found what it is that we seek.**

So what do you want? Think like a child would think. Give no thought to what is realistic, give no thought to what you believe possible. What is your dream life? Think about things like,

· Relationships, friends, romance, colleagues at work.

· Work. What is your dream job?

· Finances. How much money do you want?

· Happiness and joy. Define it.

· Accommodation. How do you want to live? Where?

· Cars and toys. Again what do you want?

· Travel and recreation. Where? 1st class?

· Family. What are you family goals?

This may all seem pie in the sky, but we have to start somewhere. Seeing things in our imagination is the start of the process. It may seem silly, but the more we think of these things, the closer they will move towards us. What we see as realistic is our very best thermostat setting and is probably close to what we currently have. Make every effort to begin to see these dreams as possible.

· **Let go of the details, they are not your concern.** We don't need to know how the impossible is going to become possible, we just need to believe that it is!

· **Raise your expectations of life.** Successful people think big. The closer your thought process can become to that of a child, the better. **Children know how to be happy – follow their example.** Seek what you want, not what you think is realistic. This is what children do. Remember that all things are possible. If you expect more from life, you will get more from life.

· **Be grateful for what you have. I do not have all I want, but I want all I have.** This attitude will definitely increase you. To desire more is fine, but only if you have already made maximum use of what you already have. There is no contradiction here.

You can be content, satisfied and happy with what you have, whilst at the same time desiring much more. You grow, become bigger and need greater resources to express that growth and to fulfil your purpose. **Take all you want, but use all you take.**

We are either growing or dying. Life seeks more life. As we attract what we are, so does life. Everything with life in it is growing constantly. Therefore, the more life we grow within us, and quicker we grow it, the more life we attract to ourselves. To maximise this growth we need resources. Life gives those resources freely and happily. The more we grow, the more life grows. It is in everybody's best interest that we increase.

Do not be fooled into thinking that we are best serving life by remaining poor; we are not. When I say poor, I mean poor in spirit, in joy, in relationships and happiness, as well as in material wealth.

The greatest thing you can do for all is to truly become wealthy in every area of your life. This way you have something to give.

By understanding these things and accepting them as truth you will begin to raise our settings. Slowly but surely you will see improvement throughout your life. Keep in mind you are battling against a lifetime of programming and indoctrination and this could take some time. Persistence and determination will ultimately win through. Stay strong, keep fighting – Good luck!

Chapter 9

Goal setting

The ability to set and achieve goals is one of the most valuable skills a person can learn. Without this almost nothing is possible. We must learn to ask and we must learn to receive. When we accomplish this, all that we desire from life becomes available to us. Thus far we have only really worked on our ability to receive, without this, asking is pointless; we have no place to put what it is that we ask for when it comes. Hopefully we have taken the time to do this and we are well prepared. Now we must learn how to ask for what it is that we want. We ask in the form of goals. If we have no goals then we have asked for nothing; this is precisely what we shall receive. It is faithful to our request and never fails.

If we ask for nothing, then it should be no surprise when we receive nothing. We must ask for a lot –everything we desire – and we must learn to do so in a way that guarantees success.

Successful, committed goal setting guarantees results.

This is almost magical! I do not have an explanation as to how it works; it doesn't really matter. Neither you nor I need to understand to the "whys" in order to benefit. All we need to know is that it does work and how to work it. **Get this right and we're**

going to have everything we want.

In order for us to be happy, we all must meet certain basic needs.

These needs are common to all in the same way that we need to eat, and we need to sleep. There are no exceptions to this. Our differences arise in how we go about meeting these needs, not in the needs themselves. As I have said repeatedly, happiness is an internal state and is not material dependant.

To be truly happy though and not to acquire the material is virtually impossible; the material is a by-product. Let me explain further.

In order to be fulfilled we all need to feel a

sense of accomplishment, achievement and growth.

As we discussed before, all things in life are either growing or dying. If we do not feel as though we are growing, then by default we feel as though we are dying. This is not compatible with happiness. So, to set and achieve financial goals, business goals, security goals and other achievements, growth goals then become essential. Not that we need money and success to be happy – we don't, but we need to feel the sense of growth that achievement of those goals brings. Do you see how it works? **We are seeking the internal, but are doing so by interacting with the external.** It can be no other way.

Another basic need is purpose. When we find and act upon our purpose in life, success can be the only result. A man or woman living a purposeful life will get up early, go to bed late, and be passionate and enthusiastic about the whole day in between. They will attract every good thing. Again, it's not every good thing that we are seeking – it is purpose – but we are going to accept and enjoy these good things as they come into our lives. Likewise, we need love, we need to contribute and we need to be valued – all basic needs. Set goals and act in such a way to meet these basic needs and it is impossible to not align our internal state of happiness and our external reality of material wealth. This is healthy and right.

Setting goals that support who we are, whilst

at the same time meeting our physical and emotional needs, brings all this together in one neat little package. Again, **we can have it all.**

I would encourage all at this point to seek further material on goal setting. There are numerous books and courses available on the subject that are excellent and go into much more detail. This is just an overview. The more you seek on the subject, the better your results are going to be. For now, let's cover some basic points:

1. So what is a goal? A goal is a dream with a deadline; a definite purpose we commit to achieving. To go another step further, a goal is a logically organised request for what it is that we want. So what do we need to do for this to work

2. Clarity. Mixed signals get mixed results. We have got to be clear about what we really want – this is essential.

3. Discipline. Physical action and work are required. We must resolve in our mind to do this, and allow nothing to stand in our way.

4. Patience. The universe, like people, does not respond to demand. What we have asked for will be given at the appropriate time. Be grateful for any perceived delays; they're in our best interest. All things happen for a good reason and all things are working in our best interest. Learn this and patience becomes much easier; even pleasant.

5. A willingness to pay the price. Nothing is free. Determine what it is that we are willing to give in order to receive what we desire. I'm not talking about money; I mean in terms of service, benefit, value and contribution. How will we use what we have asked for to leave the world a better place than we found it? We must pay, and we must negotiate the price prior to receiving.

6. Unshakeable faith that we shall receive what we have asked for. If a goal is the seed, then faith is the water that waters that seed.

We must have it. Without unshakeable faith we will fail. We will not have the necessary motivation needed to act in such a way to bring about the desired results. Total belief, regardless of the apparent impossibility of the task ahead, is mandatory. It is faith that allows us to tackle the impossible and discover for ourselves that **the impossible was only an illusion.**

7. Write it down and put a date on it. Do this and review it regularly. I can't overstate the importance of this. We must write our goals on paper, put a date for completion, and review our progress regularly. Miss this step and we will fail.

8. Think big; the bigger the better. The only way we will learn we are capable of greatness is to set and achieve great goals. However, we do have to believe we can achieve the goals we have set, so don't be stupid with this, but definitely push ourselves. This is a building process and we will soon learn that we are capable of achieving any goal. Don't sell ourselves short. Ask for what it is that we really want.

9. Do not concern ourselves with the details. We do not have to know the hows. This will become apparent at the appropriate time. Our job is simply to set the goals, and then act upon information as it comes to us. **We only ever need to know our next step.**

10. Act on information as we receive it. We do have a physical responsibility in the process.

11. Set goals seeking guidance. Not just things. Set a goal seeking guidance on setting goals.

If we do these things our life will begin to change for the better. Our goals will almost magically start to achieve themselves.

This is where the rubber hits the road. Everything so far so far has been like buying a car, getting a driving licence, putting fuel in, and so on. All that is left to do is to decide where to drive to. This is what goals are – our destination. Setting goals is simply choosing where we are going next. It's our choice. We are in control; let's take maximum advantage of the fact.

Chapter 10

Putting it all together

We are now in possession of all we need to at least make a good start in the right direction. This work is designed to be simply that; a start. It is by no means exhaustive.

Personal development is continuous and life long. The more we develop ourselves, the more capacity we develop to enjoy life to its fullest. We will be given as much in life as we are capable of using and enjoying; not a drop more or less.

Let's increase our capacity to use and enjoy.

Remember, information without action is nothing. There is no difference between one who cannot act and one who does not act. It is consistent action that will make the difference; being aware of a particular course of action that is available to us. Simply reading words will not change a single thing.

Act where we stand, begin where we are, do not wait for a better time and opportunity – there is never a better time than now. Seek as many books, programs, seminars, audio courses as we can. We simply cannot study this subject too much. The more we give to this, the more we will get back. This is our lives – make them big and exciting.

· **Become obsessed.** Obsession is generally

looked at as an unhealthy thing but that is not necessarily true. Become obsessed with the right things, with areas that will benefit and prosper us, and that's great thing.

· **Be driven.** How important is becoming happy to us? This pursuit is the most selfless, considerate cause any individual can undertake. Our happiness will make our parents happy; it will make our children happy; it will make anyone who cares about us happy. We will gain far more to give than we could ever imagine. Do not let anybody tell us that we are being selfish; they do not know what they are talking about! Let this be about us.

· **Eliminate all sources of negativity.** Newspapers, television and radio, news, negative people – everything. Knowing about all that is bad in the world does not help a single soul. Improving yourself, so that we can contribute more, does. Being aware of negative situations that we have no power to change is counter productive. It will only slow our progress in developing yourself into a person that has the ability to bring about change. Negativity of any kind will rapidly slow our progress. Make every effort to avoid it.

· **Be grateful for everything.** Gratitude is the currency of happiness. Let's have a big fat gratitude bank account so we can buy lots of happiness.

· **Learn to see the beauty and joy in everything.** It's there, just take a little time to seek it out. Spend as much time as close to nature as possible. Slow down, breathe it in. Go for a walk in the country – even better, exercise. It is all going to immeasurably help.

· **Be realistic in your time frame.** This is a long term investment. Of course, there will immediate benefit, but our real benefit will be seen over a period of years; not weeks or months. All things are possible to us, but in a realistic time frame. Most over estimate what can be achieved in one year and under estimate what can be achieved in ten years. Do not fall into this trap. Be realistic and we will have much more in the final analysis.

· **Be ambitious.** Being realistic does not

mean do not be ambitious. Always push yourself, always expect more. Set big goals, have big dreams. Desire more from life much more. We can be grateful for all we have and still want much, much more. No contradiction here. It is when we are ungrateful for what we have and desire more, we run into difficulty.

· **Eat a good diet.** We are what we eat. Our body is ours until the end. Do not ruin it by a careless diet. I have no advice on what to eat, just simply take good care of yourself. We can all find the information we need to do this.

· **Don't settle for less than everything.** And that's the minimum requirement. What we are willing to settle for is what we will end up with every time. Do not sell yourself short. Decide exactly what it is that we want – then go get it. That's all there is to it. No excuses, no stories – only results. As I have said before, life loves to wheel and deal, go strike a bargain and have all we want.

So that is all.

We have come to an end.

Thank you for reading and the very best of luck. I hope this has been helpful and I hope you personally find what it is you seek.

Keep looking and much happiness to all.

About Cody Butler

Cody Butler is one of the world's leading Educators and Motivational Speakers and on Mental Health, Anxiety, Stress and Depression.

Cody works with Clients Implementing the philosophies contained within this book to transform lives from the inside out, creating Happiness, Wealth, Health, and Joy.

He is available for personal mentorship, corporate training and as a Keynote Speaker. He also offers exclusive "Masterminds" and "Retreats" for qualified persons.

To book Cody or to learn more email

support@CodyButler.com

www.ingramcontent.com/pod-product-compliance
Ingram Content Group UK Ltd.
Pitfield, Milton Keynes, MK11 3LW, UK
UKHW022019190726
13853UKWH00005B/2010